JUICING FOR BEGINNERS

Feel Great Again With These 50 Weight Loss Juice Recipes!

(2nd edition)

Gerard Hamilton

Medical Disclaimer: The ideas and suggestions contained in this book are not intended as a substitute for consulting with your physician. All matters regarding your health require medical supervision.

Legal Disclaimer: all photos used in this book are either owned by the author, licensed for commercial use to the author, or in the public domain.

Table of Contents

PART 2: HOW TO JUICE

Why do a Juice Fast?
How to Prepare For a Juice Fast
Staying Motivated During a Juice Fast
How to Break Your Juice Fast Safely

PART 3: JUICING RECIPES

Introduction

"Let food be your medicine, and medicine be your food."

Hippocrates

Key Takeaway: *Your body is a powerful organism. Like a sports car, if you give it the right fuel, it can do magical things. If you start juicing, you are taking back control of your health. In this book you will learn everything you need to know to start your juicing journey!*

I want to thank you for buying this book, *'Juicing For Beginners: Feel Great Again With These 50 Weight Loss Juice Recipes!'*.

Take a moment and imagine the following: you are 100 pounds overweight. When you look in the mirror in the morning, you can't help but notice that your gut has the size of one of those swim rings little children play with in the pool. And on top of that, you are suffering from an autoimmune disease that is debilitating you. Every day, you take a cocktail of prescribed meds and you feel low on energy most of the day. Recently, your doctor has warned you that if you do not change your diet, you are at high risk of getting a heart attack soon.

Terrifying, right?

That's the situation the Australian Joe Cross was in when he made a radical change: he decided to only drink fresh fruit and vegetable juice for 60 days while road tripping the US, and document it for which later became the 2010 documentary 'Fat, Sick & Nearly Dead'. If you haven't seen it yet, I highly recommend you check it out!

Over the course of these 60 days, Joe lost a staggering 82 pounds! And not only that, he also lost all of the symptoms of his autoimmune disease, chronic urticaria, and was able to decrease his medicine dosage.

This experiment shows how juicing can save your life, and help you lose a lot of weight in the process.

***

According to the American Heart Association, nearly 70% of American adults are either overweight or obese. This excess weight increases the risk of all kinds of health problems such as high blood pressure, stroke, heart disease, diabetes and more.

If you start juicing, you are able to **take back control of your health**.

With this book, you will learn how you can improve your health and regain your energy levels by drinking healthy juices. And you don't need to go on a 60-day juice fast to reap the benefits. By simply incorporating healthy juices in your diet, you will be able to greatly increase the amount of nutrients from vegetables you consume.

Juicing is a fantastic way to increase your daily consumption of nutrients from veggies by three or four times.

Juicing can change your life in so many ways:

- Weight Loss
- Promoting Healthy Eating Habits
- Stop Getting Colds
- Increased Energy
- Increased Mental Clarity and Focus
- Preventing or Reversing Diabetes type 2

And all of this can be achieved in a natural way!

If you let food be your daily fuel, your medicine as Hippocrates said, you supercharge your body. And then the magic starts to work.

Your body is like a Ferrari: you need to give it the right fuel to perform well. Ferraris can't race on beer. But if you fill it up with the right gasoline, *oh boy*, you better buckle your seat belts!

That's why I'm thrilled to be writing this book, and that you are reading it. I'm really excited that you have chosen to take control of your health by picking up this book to learn about juicing. And rest assured: you have made the right choice!

In this book, I will teach you all that you need to know to start juicing. Here are some things we will cover:

- The basics of juicing
- The difference between juicing and blending
- How to pick the best juicer
- How to make a juice
- The top 10 vegetables to juice
- A TON of juicing recipes for all seasons
- And much, much more...

Sound good?

Then let's get started!

PART 1

JUICING - THE BASICS

1. What is Juicing

"Bad men live that they may eat and drink, whereas good men eat and drink that they may live."

Socrates

Key Takeaway: Juicing is the process of extracting juice from fruit and vegetables. Although it has become increasingly popular in recent years, it is not just a hype. There is documented evidence that people have been juicing for thousands of years.

Introduction

It seems to be the latest 'talk of the town': juicing.

Perhaps you have a colleague who can't keep her mouth shut about the healthy vegetable juice that she is making every morning. Or maybe you have a friend who, under the shower after a workout in the gym, is fantasizing out loud about the cucumbers and apples he will juice when he gets home. Gwyneth Paltrow included a number of juicing recipes in her cookbook 'IT'S ALL GOOD: Delicious, Easy Recipes That Will Make You Look Good and Feel Great'. And in some cities, you can even find juice bars now!

So, what's the big deal with juicing? Isn't this just the next fancy, shiny health hype?

Keep on reading, and you will quickly realize that it is most definitely not.

***

What is Juicing?

Juicing is the process of **extracting juice from fruit and vegetables**.

That's simple, right?

The juice you end up with contains most of the minerals, plant chemicals and vitamins found in the whole fruit or vegetable. Juicing is not any healthier than eating whole fruit and vegetables. But by juicing them, you can consume way more of the good stuff than if you were to eat it.

Let me point out from the very start that the health benefits of juicing mostly come from juicing **vegetables**. It is okay to add a piece of fruit to your vegetables. For example, a green apple goes really well together with all kinds of green leafy vegetables in a juice. However, fruit juices miss some things that make a whole fruit healthy. Most notably, it is loaded with sugar. There is a reason why fruit is called nature's candy!

But if you balance it well, let's say 80% vegetables and 20% fruit, you are going to greatly benefit from juicing.

***

The History of Juicing

Although it may seem like it only popped up recently, juicing is something that has been done for thousands of years. Early evidence of that are the Dead Sea Scrolls, believed to be dated between 300 BCE and 100 CE. These were only discovered in the 1940s. The Dead Sea Scrolls are a body of religious writings from the Essenes, a desert based Jewish community who followed a vegetarian diet. Of course, at the time they did not have any fancy juicers. But one of the Dead Sea Scroll texts recommends a *"pounded mash of pomegranate and fig"* which would result in *"profound strength and subtle form"*.

Over time, there have been many cultures that adopted a diet based on vegetables and fruit. So the idea of juicing these isn't that strange: it merely builds on the idea that eating vegetables and fruit is super healthy.

In the second half of the twentieth century, juicing started to gain popularity. Juicers became available in retail stores, nutritionists adopted it, and scientists started to show the health effects of juicing through their research.

Fast forward to today, and juicing seems to be everywhere. Athletes and UFC Fighters like Jon Jones swear by it. In March 2017, Oprah gave the entire cast and crew of the movie 'A Wrinkle In Time' a $399 juicer. And most relevant to you: a lot of people who live a regular life have incorporated juicing in their diet and experienced its many benefits.

***

Juicing is not just a hype. It has simply become popular because more and more people start to experience the health benefits of juicing, and spread the word. Soon, you will be one of them! At least, that is my wish for your you.

You may wonder: what are the benefits of juicing? That's what we will discuss next!

2. Health Benefits of Juicing

"He that eats till he is sick must fast till he is well."

English Proverb

Key Takeway: *Fruit and vegetables contain a lot of healthy nutrients. Through juicing you increase your fruit and vegetable nutrient intake. Juicing results in many health benefits. It slows down aging, makes you look better, helps you lose weight, increases your energy level, and boosts your immune system.*

Introduction

An average adult should consume:

- two to three servings of fruit, and
- three to five servings of vegetables a day

At least, that is what many nutritionists, doctors, and government agencies recommend.

According to the Centers for Disease Control and Prevention (CDC):

*"Compared to people who eat only small amounts of fruit and vegetables, those who eat more generous amounts — as part of a healthy diet — are likely to have **reduced risk of***

chronic diseases. *These diseases include stroke, Type 2 diabetes, some types of cancer and perhaps heart disease.*"

How many servings do *you* eat per day?

You are probably not surprised when I tell you that most people don't come anywhere close to these recommendations.

But here is the **health hack**: juicing provides an effective and simple way to meet your dietary requirements for fresh fruit and vegetables! Just adding one glass of fresh juice to your daily diet can make all the difference!

Sounds good, right?

But wait, there is more. Juicing is not only good for disease prevention. In this chapter, we are going to take a quick look at all the many benefits of juicing.

***

Juicing Slows Down Aging

As you grow older, your body starts to lose strength and energy. Grey hairs appear, or you may even start to lose hair.

An important cause of aging are free radicals, which damage cells. As a result, these cells become more vulnerable to premature aging and disease. This process cannot be prevented entirely, aging is inherent to life. But what you can do is feed the cells nutrients of the highest quality. This will strengthen them, and enable them to perform at an optimal level. Remember the Ferrari analogy?

Fruit and vegetables are full of those superpower nutrients. And if you juice them, you are not only able to consume more of the good stuff per day, your body will also absorb the nutrients more easily. How does this work?

As years go by, your digestive system starts taking hits from all the toxins that enter your body as a result of all the bad foods you eat. Think KFC, muffins and soft drinks. This impairs your body's ability to properly digest the food you eat and absorb all its nutrients. Even if it's healthy food! But by juicing the food, you have already done most of the digesting before you even take your first sip. Compare it to baby food: because of its soft texture, it is easier for the baby to digest. By juicing fruit and vegetables, you allow the nutrients to pass directly into your bloodstream. It's like injecting natural doping!

***

Juicing Makes You Look Better

As you start to juice on a daily basis, you will notice that your skin starts to improve. Your skin is one of the biggest bodily organs, and consists of three layers:

- **Epidermis**: this is the outer layer, which provides a waterproof barrier to external toxins and chemicals, as well as the sun's rays. It also gives your skin its color.

- **Dermis**: this deeper layer provides the epidermis with new cells, as dead cells are flaked off its surface. It produces oil to keep your skin soft, it grows hair and produces sweat.
- **Hypodermis**: this is the deepest layer. Among other things, it stores fat and controls your body temperature.

The nutrients in fruit and vegetables, as well as the water in them, improve the quality of the cells in your skin. During the first days of a juice fast, you may see some acne or pimples pop up, but that is a good sign: your skin is going through a process of purification, expelling toxins. But shortly after, you will start noticing your skin transforming. It will start glowing more, while wrinkles and facial lines are lessening.

And the effects of juicing on your body doesn't stop there. Your hair and nails, which are directly connected to your skin, will also become stronger and begin to shine more.

Who doesn't want to look good? With juicing, you will not only feel healthier, but you'll also be welcomed by a prettier face in the mirror in the morning. Plus, you will be able to save a lot of money on all kinds of beauty products, yay!

***

Juicing Helps You Lose Weight

In the introduction of this book, I told you how Joe Cross lost 82 pounds in 60 days of juice fasting. And I have personally lost 13 pounds a number of years ago when I did a 10-day juice fast. And the best thing is: most of it stayed off, after I returned to a normal diet!

Losing weight is simply a matter of burning more calories than you take in. Your body will then start using the fat already stored in your body as fuel, and burn it. Fruit and vegetables contain carbohydrates and plant proteins, but no fat. Just a reminder: fat isn't categorically bad for you. Your body needs a small amount of healthy fats, especially Omega-3 fats are good for you. These can be found in foods like salmon, walnuts and soybeans. However, by building your diet around fruit and vegetables, you will keep your fat intake low.

Just by replacing eating potato chips or Oreo cookies with drinking a green smoothie, the pounds will start flying off!

***

Juicing Increases Your Energy Level

To perform at an optimal level, your body needs to be in a prime state. And the way to get there is to give it what it needs: high-quality nutrients. Juicing is one of the best ways of doing so. Juiced fruit and vegetables contain the building blocks of healthy cells, such as vitamins, potassium and antioxidants. And because you juice them, they are injected in the bloodstream almost immediately after you drink it. You will be able to think more clearly, feel more vital, your memory improves, and you will feel better about yourself.

There is even a mental effect. I like to jog in the park. When I get tired, I try to pump myself up again and keep going. One way of doing that is by simply raising my arms in the air, like athletes do when they win a race. But another thing I have experimented with is visualizing a healthy juice. And the effect is really interesting: when I visualize French fries, or other unhealthy foods, my energy level drops even further. But when I visualize a healthy green smoothie, it energizes me. Try it out for yourself!

***

Juicing Boosts Your Immune System

Your body is an impressive superorganism. It is exposed to a variety of toxins, bacteria and viruses every day, yet you don't get sick most of the time. Why is that? Because of your powerful immune system. The immune system is the body's first line of defense, and it keeps most unwelcome visitors out.

The stronger your immune system, the better it can perform. And the less sick you will be. Fruit and vegetables are jam-packed with phytochemicals. These are chemicals that plants produce to protect themselves. But they can also prevent, or mitigate the effects of, diseases in humans. So, by juicing fruit and vegetables, you are strengthening your immune system, and laying the foundation for a healthy life.

Additionally, juicing is also great to detox the body, especially if you do a juice fast. Juicing allows your body to clear waste from the digestive system and your liver, as well as rid your body of all kinds of toxins.

***

Now you know the most important health benefits of juicing. But what do you need to make a juice? You will need a powerful juicer that is able to distract all the nutrients from the fruit and vegetables, without crushing them. That's why I recommend you use a proper juicer, and not a blender.

Next up, you will learn the difference between a juicer and a blender.

3. The Difference Between Juicing and Blending

"Nature itself is the best physician."

Hippocrates

Key Takeaway: *Juices are made with a juicer, and smoothies with a blender. Juices are more nutrient dense and of higher nutritional quality per serving. Blended smoothies contain more fiber contained in fruit and vegetables, and can be mixed with other foods, such as nuts and seeds.*

Introduction

There is a distinct difference between juicing and blending. Juices are made with a juicer, smoothies are made with a blender. Here are some of the differences between the two.

***

A Juice is of Higher Quality Than a Blended Smoothie

A juicer extracts the juice out of fruit and vegetables, and separates the pulp from the juice. Most juicers extract the juice at a slow pace, to minimize damaging the produce, resulting in a high-quality juice. A juicer gives you a nutrient-dense drink that is smaller than a blended smoothie, while still containing most of the nutrients.

A blender on the other hand pulverizes the fruit and vegetables. There is no left-over pulp. The blender's sharp high rotation blades, and the heat they create, can damage the nutrients in fruit and vegetables, resulting in a lower quality drink.

***

Juices Don't Contain Fiber, Blended Smoothies Do

Because the pulp is separated from the juice, the juice hardly contains any fiber. The benefit is that all the nutrients are sent into the bloodstream directly. The fiber in smoothies slows down the absorption of these nutrients, and some nutrients leave your body again because they stay in the fiber.

Don't get me wrong: fiber helps with digestion and it slows down the absorption of sugar. You shouldn't exclude fiber from your diet altogether. But it is perfectly fine to do a juice fast and minimize fiber consumption for a while, giving your digestive tract a well-deserved rest to detox. And if you are on a healthy diet, you will already consume enough fiber, so you won't miss the additional fiber in the juiced fruit and vegetables anyway.

***

Juices Are More Nutrient Dense Per Glass

Because a juicer separates the pulp from the liquid, juices are smaller in size than blended smoothies. Therefore, one glass of juice contains more nutrients than a blended smoothie of the same size.

***

Juices Are Pure Extracts, Blended Smoothies Can Be Mixed With Nuts and Seeds

Where a juice is a pure extract of the nutrients in fruit and vegetables, smoothies can be blended more easily with other foods such as nuts, seeds or even yoghurt. This is mostly because of the blender's high-power rotation blades. This creates a drink that contains more proteins and fats. It will be thicker than a juice.

***

So, which one is better? Many of the health benefits of juicing also apply to blended smoothies. However, in general, juicing gives faster results. A juice is a pure extract, and contains more nutrients per serving than a blended smoothie. The quality of a juice is higher than that of a blended smoothie. And juicing is a great way to detox your body, because the nutrients are easily absorbed, giving your digestive system a rest.

But you can't really go wrong here. A blended smoothie is always a healthier option than a coke or pancakes with maple syrup. So feel free to mix things up, and change your juice for a smoothie every once in a while!

4. What to Look for When Buying a Juicer

"Our bodies are our gardens – our wills are our gardeners."

William Shakespeare

Key Takeaway: *There are two types of juicers: masticating and centrifugal. The juice pressed by a masticating juicer is of a higher quality than that of a centrifugal juicer. They can be differentiated in two ways: (1) Type of screw: single gear or twin gear, and (2) Type of press: horizontal or vertical.*

Which masticating juicer to choose depends on your wants and needs. Twin gear masticating juicers are for real juice fanatics. For everyone else the single gear masticating juicer is the best option. And although horizontal masticating juicers are better equipped to press wheatgrass, vertical masticating juicers are the best option for most people because they press the juice faster without loss of quality.

Introduction

I hope you are excited about juicing by now! But how do you get started? Well, to make a juice, you need a juicer.

There are different types of juicers on the market. Which one should you buy?

In this chapter, you will learn the difference between a masticating juicer and a centrifugal juicer, and why I recommend you choose the former over the latter. And I will explain the different types of masticating juicers, so you can pick the one that is right for you.

***

Masticating Juicers vs Centrifugal Juicers

Juicers come in two types:

- Centrifugal juicers
- Masticating juicers

There are four main differences between the two:

1. Rotation Speed
2. Juice Quality
3. Price
4. Sound Level

Let's take a look at each of them.

1. Rotation Speed

The first difference is the rotation speed.

A masticating juicer juices vegetables and fruit at a low rotation, typically 40-80 rounds per minute. It uses a screw that bruises the produce, and then squeezes the juice out.

A centrifugal juicer, on the other hand, resembles a centrifuge in your laundry machine. The vegetables and fruit are rotated at a high rotation speed and cut by a razor-sharp grater, almost at the speed of a blender.

Because a masticating juicer rotates at a lower speed, the juicing will take a little bit longer. However, the time difference is minor.

2. Juice Quality

A second difference is the quality of the juice.

The juice made in a masticating juicer is of a higher quality than that made in a centrifugal juicer. The high rotation speed of a centrifugal juicer creates heat and friction, which leads to oxidation. This has a negative influence on the quality of the juice. The low rotation speed of a masticating juicer creates little to no heat and hardly any oxidation. This is why you can keep the juice for 1-2 days in a closed bottle in your fridge. If a juice is made with a centrifugal juicer, it is better to drink it immediately.

3. Price

The third difference is the price.

Centrifugal juicers and masticating juicers are available in various price categories. Generally, a centrifugal juicer will be somewhat cheaper than a masticating juicer. But you get what you pay for. Investing in a quality juicer always pays off.

Make sure you do your research before buying either a masticating juicer or a centrifugal juicer. And don't just focus on the price.

4. Sound Level

The last difference is the sound level.

Similar to a blender, a centrifugal juicer can produce quite a lot of noise, while a masticating juicer produces very little. This is caused by the difference in rotation speed.

If you use a masticating juicer, you can have a conversation at the same time. This is not really possible when you use a centrifugal juicer.

***

How to Choose the Best Masticating Juicer

A masticating juicer gives the highest quality juice, so I recommend choosing it over a centrifugal juicer. But which masticating juicer should you buy?

Roughly speaking, there are two ways in which masticating juicers can be differentiated:

1. **Type of screw: single gear or twin gear**
2. **Type of press: horizontal or vertical**

A single gear can press both horizontally or vertically. However, all twin gear masticating juicers press horizontally.

Let's take a closer look at the differences.

1. Type of screw: single gear or twin gear

First, masticating juicers can be divided in single or twin gears. What is the difference?

Twin Gear

A twin gear masticating juicer has two screws. An example is the Greenstar Elite:

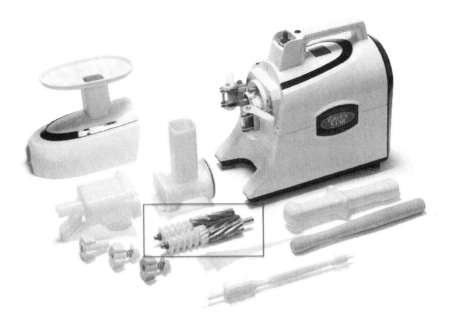

Do you see the two screws?

Twin gear masticating juicers are primarily popular with professional users and the real juice fanatics. These masticating juicers will give the best possible juice that a masticating juicer can press.

A double screw breaks down the ingredients more thoroughly compared to a single gear masticating juicer. This makes a twin gear ideal for juicing wheatgrass. However, twin gears are quite expensive. Also, they are more difficult to clean.

Single Gear

Most masticating juicers are single gear. These masticating juicers are equipped with a single screw.

An example is this Hurom juicer:

For most people, a single gear masticating juicer is the best option. A single gear masticating juicer is easier to use and also easier to clean. Moreover, the quality of a juice made in a single gear masticating juicer hardly differs from that of a twin gear. Add to that a lower price, and you can see why single gear juicers are so popular.

To recap:

- A twin gear masticating juicer is for professional users and real juice fanatics.
- For everyone else, the single gear masticating juicer is the best option.

2. Type of press: horizontal or vertical

Another way in which masticating juicers can be differentiated is the way in which the juice is pressed: horizontally or vertically.

Not too long ago, all masticating juicers pressed horizontally. Recently though, more and more vertical juicers have entered the market. What is the difference between the two?

Horizontal press

In a horizontal juicer, the funnel entrance is positioned in a right angle to the engine axis. An example is the Sana 707:

A horizontal juicer is better equipped for juicing wheatgrass than a vertical juicer. However, a disadvantage of a horizontal juicer is that, often, you need to push the ingredients through the funnel. Also, it will cost more time to press the juice than with its vertical brother.

Vertical press

Since the vertical masticating juicer entered the market a few years ago, it has become very popular in a short amount of time. That is because vertical juicers press faster, without diminishing the quality of the juice. Here is how this works.

To reduce the amount of time in which ingredients are pressed to juice, increasing the rotation speed is not an option. This would cause friction and heat, and thus reduce the quality of the juice.

So how can the press speed be increased? By increasing the amount of ingredients that can be juiced with every rotation. For this, a bigger juice surface is required: a bigger screw and a bigger filter. This is problematic with a masticating juicer that presses the juice horizontally. Because the funnel entrance is positioned in a right angle to the engine axis, the possibilities to change the size and weight of the various parts are limited.

A vertical juicer, however, does not have this limitation: the funnel entrance and motor axis are positioned in a straight line. This makes it possible to equip the masticating juicer with a bigger press screw and filter. The effect is that, with each rotation, more ingredients are juice-pressed.

To recap:

- A horizontal masticating juicer is best if you want to juice wheatgrass.
- A vertical juicer is easier to use for all other fruit and vegetables, as it presses the juice faster, without loss of quality.

***

Now you know the difference between masticating and centrifugal juicers, and the different types of masticating juicers.

The juice pressed by a masticating juicer is of a higher quality than that of a centrifugal juicer. Which masticating juicer you should buy depends on your wants and needs.

Horizontal twin gear masticating juicers are for professionals and real juice fanatics. For most other people though, the vertical single gear masticating juicer is the best option.

PART 2

HOW TO JUICE

5. How to Make a Juice

"Plant a radish, get a radish, never any doubt. That's why I love vegetables, you know what they're about!"

Tom Jones

Key Takeaway: *making a juice is quite easy. Make sure to only use high-quality fruit and vegetables, wash them before use and cut them into small pieces before putting them into the feeding tube. Happy juicing!*

Introduction

Once you have picked your favorite juicer and bought it, you are ready to make your first juice! This book contains a bunch of tasty and healthy recipes to get you started. And really, juicing is not hard to do. Just follow the juicing tips in this chapter!

Only Use High-Quality Produce

In order to reap the most health benefits from your juice, make sure you only pick high-quality ingredients.

A lot of farmers use synthetic pesticides and fertilizers, to grow fruit and vegetables faster, and to keep parasites away. Consuming these toxins is not healthy.

Instead, opt for organic produce. Farmers who use the organic approach to grow their fruit and vegetables do not use any synthetic pesticides or fertilizers, and instead use more natural alternatives. Although it may take longer before the fruit and vegetables are ready to harvest, they are much healthier to consume.

Tip: The label "organic" is not the same as "natural". Generally speaking, the food label "natural" does not refer to how the food was grown. It just means that it does not contain any artificial colors, flavors or preservatives.

Try to keep a balance of 80-100% vegetables, and a maximum of 20% fruit. The real health benefits come from the vegetables, but you can add some fruit for flavor. Apple goes especially well with green, leafy vegetables.

***

Wash Before Use

Always wash your fruit and veggies before use, even if you use organic produce. Especially if you use the peel, for example of a beetroot, a carrot or ginger. You can't know for sure what happened to them when they were grown, and it's better to be safe than sorry. Also, you don't want any sand in your juice, so make sure to clean your fruit and vegetables before you put them in the juicer.

***

Cut the Fruit/Vegetables into Small Pieces

Unlike a blender, the juicer's feeding tube is quite small. And on top of that, masticating juicers press the fruit and vegetables at a low speed. If you don't cut that beetroot or carrot, the screw may get stuck.

The best way to go about this is to cut your produce:

- into pieces of 1 - 1.5 inches, or
- lengthwise. This mostly works for vegetables like cucumbers, carrots and celery

***

Turn on the Juicer

You are now ready to start juicing! Turn on the juicer. If you haven't used it for a few days, first pour a cup of water in the feeding tube, to clean it. Then throw the water away.

***

Put the Pieces in The Juicer

Put the pieces in the feeding tube of the juicer, one by one. Take your time, don't push the ingredients in there all at once. The screw may get stuck if you do.

If you use different ingredients, such as spinach, apple and kale, alternate putting them in the juicer. This way they mix best, creating the best flavor for your juice!

***

Put the Pulp Back in the Juicer

After you have juiced all the pieces, you should have a lot of pulp. You can extract some extra juice out of this pulp by putting it back into the feeding tube, juicing it again.

***

Drink or Store the Juice

Your juice is now ready! It is best to drink it immediately.

If you have made more than one glass and want to store some, pour it into a (preferably glass) container and close it. A fresh juice can be stored for up to two days in the fridge. Just remember that a fresh juice contains the most nutrients, so if you have enough time it is best to make your juice fresh.

***

Clean the Juicer

Don't forget to clean your juicer as soon as you have finished your juice! Read the juicer's manual to check if the parts can be placed in a dishwasher. It is best to wash the parts with warm water and a brush. It is not necessary to use dish soap. If you do use it, wash it thoroughly. You don't want your next juice to taste a bit off...

***

That is how you make a juice. Not that difficult, right?

Next up, we are going to cover the top 10 vegetables to juice, so you know which ones to pick when you start making your own juices!

6. Top 10 Best Vegetables to Juice

"Shipping is a terrible thing to do to vegetables. They probably get jet-lagged, just like people."

Elizabeth Berry

Key Takeaway: The 10 vegetables in this chapter all have spectacular health benefits. However, don't limit yourself to these: half of the fun in juicing is trying out new combinations!

Introduction

You can't go wrong when juicing vegetables: they are all healthy! But to keep juicing fun, it is best to try to combine different vegetables. Not only does each vegetable have its own distinct flavor, it also has its own unique combination of nutrients.

Below are the top 10 best vegetables to juice:

1. Beets
2. Bell Pepper
3. Broccoli
4. Carrot
5. Celery

6. Cucumber
7. Ginger
8. Kale
9. Spinach
10. Wheatgrass

These vegetables are all really good for you. So definitely make them a staple in your juice repertoire!

***

1. Beets

Sometimes the beauty found in nature beats anything created by man. Slicing a beet in half and taking in the deep red color can be a mesmerizing experience.

Beets are unique in that they are one of the best sources of phytonutrients called betalains. These are excellent in providing anti-inflammatory and antioxidant support, boosting your immune system.

Fun fact: *The biggest beet ever grown weighed over 156 pounds! It was grown by Piet de Goede, a Dutchman.*

Furthermore, beets are rich in folate, manganese, potassium, copper, and are also a great source of magnesium, phosphorus, vitamins B6 and C8, as well as iron.

The health benefits of beets include:

- Promotes optimal health
- Reduces inflammation
- Boosts immune system
- Great for detoxification
- Reduces risk of many types of cancer

***

2. Bell Pepper

Bell peppers come in a wide variety of beautiful colors and are beautifully shaped, almost as if they were designed to be Christmas tree ornaments!

The red, orange and yellow bell peppers have a fruity and sweet flavor, whereas the green and purple ones are slightly more bitter.

Fun fact: *although they may look like vegetables, bell peppers are actually fruit. Why? Because they grow on flowering plants and have seeds!*

Bell peppers contain one of the highest levels of carotenoids. These are pigments that not only give the vegetable their color, but are also antioxidants associated with many health benefits. Bell peppers are an excellent source of Vitamin C.

And they contain a good amount of Vitamins E, B36, B26, B14 and K5, as well as folate, molybdenum, pantothenic acid, potassium, manganese, phosphorus and magnesium.

The health benefits of bell pepper include:

- Reduces inflammation
- Boosts your immune system
- Improves quality of the skin and hair
- Helps heal eyes and ward off eye disease
- Reduces bad cholesterol
- Helps prevent cancer

***

3. Broccoli

Broccoli has been eaten since the times the Romans ruled Europe, millennia ago. Its name comes from the Italian word *broccolo*, which means the flowering top of a cabbage.

Fun fact: *Thomas Jefferson is widely known as one of the founding fathers of the United States. However, he also loved gardening. He imported broccoli seeds from Italy to plant them at Monticelli, his plantation.*

This cruciferous vegetable is a powerhouse of nutrients. Broccoli is loaded with vitamins K and C. It is also rich in chromium and folate. And it contains other healthy nutrients such as pantothenic acid, vitamins A, B1, B2, B3, B6, E, phosphorus, manganese, choline, potassium, copper, as well as omega-3 fats, magnesium, protein, zinc, calcium and selenium.

The health benefits of broccoli include:

- Improves detoxification
- Can prevent certain types of cancer
- Aids digestion
- Provides cardiovascular support
- Improves eye health
- Lowers risk of type 2 diabetes

***

4. Carrot

Unlike many other vegetables, the juice of carrots tastes quite sweet. So, this is a great vegetable to add if you want to take the sharp edges of your juice!

Carrots are one of the best vegetables to consume to prevent cardiovascular disease. This was the outcome of a 10-year scientific study that looked into the health effects of fruit and vegetables in four color categories: green, white, red/purple, and orange/yellow. The last one turned out to be the most protective against cardiovascular disease. And in this category, carrots topped the chart.

Fun fact: *Have you ever heard someone say that eating large quantities of carrots will help you see in the dark? This urban legend originates in World War II. To cover up the effectiveness of their radar equipment, the RAF* *circulated the rumor that the British pilots were able to shoot down German planes at night because they ate so many carrots!*

Carrots are loaded with vitamin A. It is also a great source of biotin, vitamins B1, B2, B3, B6, E, C and K, molybdenum, potassium and manganese. And it contains pantothenic acid, copper, phosphorus and folate.

The health benefits of carrot include:

- Prevents cardiovascular disease
- Improves eye health (perhaps there is a little bit of truth in that urban legend...)
- Reduces blood pressure
- Protects teeth and gums
- Promotes skin health
- Reduces risk of several types of cancer

***

5. Celery

Celery is eaten by some as a low-calorie snack with a bite, as an alternative to more unhealthy snacks.

Fun fact: *In 1996, the English football club Gillingham FC no longer allowed fans to bring celery to the stadium. The goalie of the team was overweight, and the fans brought celery with them to the stadium to throw it at the goalie during the match...*

Celery does much more than aid in weight loss. It is rich in Vitamin K, as well as Vitamins A, B25, C4 and B64. It is also a great source of potassium, folate, molybdenum, manganese, calcium, as well as magnesium.

The health benefits of celery include:

- Reduces inflammation
- Lowers blood pressure
- Helps with weight loss
- Lowers cholesterol
- Aids digestion

***

6. Cucumber

Cucumbers are very versatile: they are excellent for face masks, tasty in a gin and tonic, and can be used to scare the living hell out of cats...

But this lengthy vegetable truly shines when added to your diet.

Fun fact: *Ever heard the expression 'cool as a cucumber'? This term is derived from the cucumber's ability to cool blood temperature and ease facial swelling when applied topically.*

Unlike many other vegetables, cucumbers contain a lot of water. That's why they are great to juice with other vegetables. They hold a good amount of vitamin K, and also contain molybdenum, pantothenic acid, potassium, phosphorus and copper, as well as manganese, vitamins C4 and B13, biotin and magnesium.

The health benefits of cucumber include:

- Improves brain health
- Reduces inflammation
- Supports digestive health
- Helps to maintain a healthy weight
- Lowers risk of certain types of cancer

***

7. Ginger

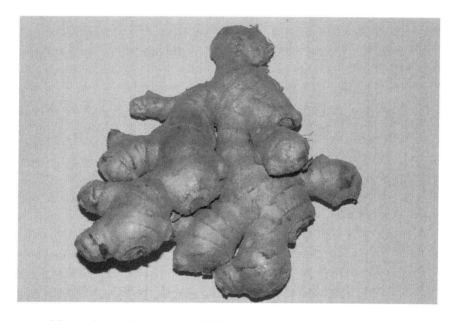

Just like salt and pepper add flavor to a steak or mashed potatoes, ginger gives a nice spicy twist to your juice. However, it is not just the taste that make this root a winner. Ginger has been used for thousands of years by the Chinese and Indians for its medicinal properties. It is especially good to treat any symptoms of gastrointestinal distress.

Fun fact: *Many centuries ago, Chinese sailors would chew on ginger to fight of seasickness. It was also used to reverse shellfish poisoning, which might be one of the reasons why today ginger is still a key ingredient in many Chinese seafood dishes.*

The most important active ingredient in ginger is gingerol, which is responsible for its many health benefits. Ginger is also rich in potassium, magnesium, phosphorus and folate.

And it contains other nutrients such as sodium, calcium, protein, vitamins B6 and C, zinc and iron.

The health benefits of ginger include:

- Aids digestion and prevents constipation
- Reduces obesity
- Decreases risk of type 2 diabetes
- Prevents heart disease
- Reduces inflammation
- Boosts the immune system
- Increases your energy level
- Helps with nausea after cancer treatment
- Helps with losing weight

***

8. Kale

Kale is not on top of everyone's list of favorite vegetables, because of its strong and slightly bitter flavor. However, this super healthy green should be a regular ingredient in your juice, because it is one of the most nutrient dense foods out there.

Fun fact: *Until its 2013 surge in popularity, the single largest consumer of kale in the U.S. was Pizza Hut, who used the leafy vegetable not for food, but to decorate its salad bars.*

Kale is an excellent source of Vitamins K, A and C. It also contains other healthy nutrients such as manganese, copper, calcium, potassium, iron, as well as vitamins B1, B2, B3, B6 and E, magnesium, protein, phosphorus, omega-3 fats and folate.

The health benefits of kale include:

- Helps lower bad cholesterol
- Reduces risk of certain types of cancer
- Promotes eye health
- Supports cardiovascular health
- Great for detoxification
- Helps infant brain development in the womb

***

9. Spinach

Spinach is rich in antioxidants and has an extremely high nutritional value. A number of scientific studies have shown that juicing spinach is actually the best way to obtain its maximum nutritional value.

Fun fact: *Popeye's claim that eating spinach gives him superior strength is based on a miscalculation by a German chemist. He calculated that 100 grams of spinach contains about 35 milligrams of iron, where in reality it is only 3.5 milligrams. However, before the error was corrected by other scientists, it had already become part of popular culture.*

Spinach is very rich in Vitamin K. And it is an excellent source of vitamin A, manganese, folate, magnesium, and iron. Moreover, it also contains copper, vitamins B1, B2, B3, B6, C and E, calcium and potassium, as well as phosphorus, zinc, protein, choline, omega-3 fats, selenium and pantothenic acid.

The health benefits of spinach include:

- Increases muscle efficiency
- Slows down aging
- Helps regulate hunger, satiety, and blood sugar levels
- Reduces inflammation
- Promotes eye health
- Reduces risk of different types of cancer, including breast, skin, prostate and ovarian cancer

***

10. Wheatgrass

Wheatgrass is nicknamed "liquid gold", because it is denser in nutrients than anything else. One serving of wheatgrass juice is roughly equivalent to 1,5 pounds of dark leafy green vegetables!

Wheatgrass has a distinct flavor, it is definitely an acquired taste. You can either juice it with other vegetables, or juice it on its own, for example if you want to start your day with a wheatgrass shot. It is best to drink wheatgrass on an empty stomach, an hour before eating anything else. This allows all the nutrients to be fully absorbed by your body.

Fun fact: *wheatgrass is gluten-free, despite the fact that it has 'wheat' in the name.*

Wheatgrass is rich in chlorophyll, antioxidants like flavonoids and phenolic acid, iron, and electrolytes such as magnesium and calcium. It also contains a lot of amino acids, vitamins A, C and E, as well as selenium.

Wheatgrass has more health benefits than anything else you can juice. It:

- Strengthens the immune system
- Slows down aging
- Eases pain of rheumatism and arthritis
- Reduces risk of different types of cancer
- Purifies the liver
- Promotes digestive health
- Helps regulate blood sugar
- Fights skin conditions such as psoriasis and eczema
- Helps with sleep
- Aids digestion, and helps with constipation

***

These 10 vegetables are great to begin with if you are new to juicing! Whenever you are stuck for inspiration, you can go back to these time and again, and boost your vitality.

However, this is by no means a limited list. Try out any vegetable you like that is not included here. Keep surprising yourself with new flavors, and find the ones you like best!

7. How to do a Juice Fast

"Periodic fasting can help clear up the mind and strengthen the body and the spirit."

Ezra Taft Benson

Key Takeaway: *A juice fast is a fasting method in which you only consume fruit and vegetable juice. Juice fasting is a great way to detoxify your body, and can also increase your energy level and help you lose weight. To maximize your chances of success, you should prepare yourself mentally and physically for a juice fast. There will be moments of struggle. When this happens, focus on why you are doing the fast. When you have finished your fast, allow for some days to return to a healthy diet of solid foods again.*

Introduction

You now know all the basics of juicing, and how to make your own juice. You can start adding juices to your diet immediately. And to inspire you to get started, the last chapters contain a variety of recipes for healthy *and* tasty juices.

However, if you want to step it up a notch by doing a juice fast, there are certain things you need to be aware of.

***

What is a Juice Fast?

A juice fast, also known as a juice cleanse, is a fasting method in which you only consume fruit and vegetable juice. No solid food. In addition, your drinks are also restricted. Besides tea and water, all other drinks are out. No coffee, soft drinks or alcohol.

There is no fixed duration for a juice fast: it can last anywhere from just a few days to many weeks. Remember Joe Cross's 60-day fast?

To get the best effects though, a minimum duration of 5 days is recommended.

***

Why do a Juice Fast?

Doing a juice fast is like resetting your digestive system. Years of consuming fast food, beer, chips and other unhealthy foods affect your digestive tract, your liver and blood.

By doing a juice fast, you are giving your digestive system a rest. Your body is fueled with healthy nutrients, which are absorbed almost immediately after consumption. As a result, all your energy can be used to restore your body.

In addition, juice fasting has the following benefits:

- Rapid weight loss
- Increased mental clarity
- Increased energy
- Feeling more centered
- Chronic diseases that are the result of a poor diet can start to heal
- Skin starts to glow more

Juice fasting can be an intense experience though. Something you want to prepare for.

***

How to Prepare For a Juice Fast

Don't expect to feel good from the get-go. Your body is not used to drinking only healthy juices. So expect to feel a bit off the first few days.

But there are steps you can take to prepare for a soft landing:

- **Set a Clear Goal**: before you start your juice fast, decide how many days you are going to fast.
- **Write Down Why You Want to do a Juice Fast**: what is the reason for your juice fast: weight loss? Giving your digestive system a well-deserved break? Whatever it is, write it down together with your goal and stick it on your fridge. When the going gets tough, look at the piece of paper to remind yourself why you are doing this juice fast.

- **Eat Healthy Prior to Starting Your Juice Fast:** in the week before starting the fast, cut out all fast food, sugary foods and soft drinks, and replace them with (mostly) vegetables. This will make the transition from solid to liquid food a lot smoother.
- **Get in the Right Mindset**: Prepare yourself mentally for the fast. Whenever you change something in your life, you are adding some level of stress to your life. By making sure you are in a good state beforehand, you are laying the foundation of a successful juice cleanse. Exercise regularly, meditate, visualize yourself enjoying your juice fast, and picture how good you will feel after you have completed the fast.
- **Start on a Friday**: the second and third day are often the most challenging. By starting your juice fast on a Friday, those days will be in the weekend, which gives you the freedom to do whatever you want. You're not passing Dunkin' Donuts on the way to work, and if you feel like doing nothing you can just chill on the couch and watch Netflix.
- **Use the Seinfeld Technique**: When Jerry Seinfeld was asked what it takes to become a good comedian, he answered that a good comedian writes jokes every day. And the way he committed to that was by hanging a big calendar on the wall and putting a big red X over the day on which he wrote a joke. From then on, it was very simple: *"Don't break the chain."* You can do the same. If you plan a 10-day juice fast, take a piece of paper and draw a table with 10 boxes. At the end of each day, put a big X in the box for that

day. And then do the same thing the next day. And the next day…Don't break the chain!

***

Staying Motivated During a Juice Fast

The first day of your fast may still be pretty easy, as you are riding the initial wave of excitement.

However, the second and third day are usually the toughest. You will probably crave solid food. And not just any solid food, but all kinds of unhealthy foods. Think chocolate, cookies, pizza. Don't give up now! These cravings will pass.

You may also feel low on energy these first days. When this happens, make sure you drink enough juice. There is no cap on the servings you can consume. So there is really no excuse for being hungry. Just make an extra juice. Most people on a juice fast report that from day four and on, they actually feel *more* energized than on a regular diet. Keep this in mind if you feel a bit groggy in the beginning.

It is also possible that pimples start developing on your skin. No need to freak out, this is a good sign! Your body is in detox mode, expelling toxins. Pimples are a sign that your body is releasing these toxins through the skin. Be happy that your amazing body is purifying itself! And rest assured, these pimples will go away eventually.

When you feel tempted to break your fast prematurely, take a deep breath and look at your piece of paper: why did you start this juice cleanse in the first place? Focus on why you want to achieve your goal, and the sense of accomplishment you will feel upon completion. And use the Seinfeld technique to mark off every successful day.

***

How to Break Your Juice Fast Safely

Great, the juice fast is over, yay! Now let's get pizza and steak!

This is the *worst* possible thing you can do...

These last days, or even weeks, you have gone without consuming any solid food. If you feed your body with unhealthy foods now, you will not only undo some of the purification effects, but you will likely get constipated too. You need to allow for a few days to transition to a healthy diet of solid foods again.

During the fast, your stool stopped at some point, as you were only drinking liquids. Now you need to kickstart the engine again, so to speak. The way to do this is by eating only soft vegetables, or fruit that contain lots of water. Stick to fruit like melon or orange, and soft cooked vegetables. It would be best to continue drinking juice for these days. Do not eat anything that is difficult to digest, such as meat, within the first 48 hours after your juice fast. Experiment with different foods and listen to your body.

***

There you have it: the keys to the juicing castle. You know what juicing is, how to make a juice, and even how to safely do a juice fast and detox your body.

The rest of this book is filled with a bunch of delicious, healthy juice recipes. They are organized based on the four seasons: spring, summer, autumn and winter.

Ideally, you'd mostly juice fruit and vegetables that are in season.

Let's start juicing!

PART 3

JUICING RECIPES

8. Juicing Recipes - Spring

In spring, everything starts coming back to life. The circle of life begins again! This chapter contains recipes for juices that are best made in the spring.

The names of the recipes in this chapter are:

- Green Happiness
- Veggie Power
- Red Bell Pepper & Celery
- Veggie Cocktail
- Mint Refreshment
- Digestion Booster
- Kiwi Attack
- Thirst Quencher
- Rhubarb and Mint
- Carrot and Bell Pepper
- V8-copycat
- Yellow Tomato Juice
- Gazpacho Twist
- Tropical Surprise

Let's begin with the Green Happiness juice!

***

1. Green Happiness

This powerful green juice will immediately improve your mood and put a smile on your face!

Ingredients

- 2 Broccoli stalks
- 3.5 oz (125 gr.) Watercress
- ½ Cucumber
- ¼ Lemon (without peel)

Directions

- Cut the broccoli into pieces of about 1 - 1.5 inches (2 - 3 cm)
- Use both the watercress stems and leaves
- Cut the watercress stems in half
- Cut the cucumber lengthwise
- Peel the lemon, cut out a ¼ part and put the rest away
- Turn on the juicer
- Put the broccoli stalks, watercress, cucumber and lemon in the juicer, piece by piece
- End with a piece of broccoli
- Pour into a glass, serve and drink immediately

***

2. Veggie Power

Packed with healthy nutrients, this is the perfect breakfast to start the day with.

Ingredients

- 2 Winter Carrots
- 1 Celery stalk
- 1 Beetroot
- ¼ Cucumber
- Handful of Parsley

Directions

- Cut the carrot lengthwise. Then slice it into parts about the size of thick potato fries
- Cut the celery lengthwise into pieces of 1 - 1.5 inches (2 - 3 cm)
- Cut the beetroot into pieces of 0.5 - 1 inches (1 - 2 cm)
- Cut the cucumber lengthwise
- Chop the parsley
- Turn on the juicer
- Put the carrot, celery, beetroot, cucumber and parsley in the juicer, piece by piece
- The power of the juicer will pull the cucumber in automatically, absorbing the last bits of flavor in the juice
- Pour into a glass, serve and drink immediately

***

3. Red Bell Pepper & Celery

This juice combines two of the top 10 vegetables recommended earlier in this book. A real powerhouse!

Ingredients

- 1 red Bell Pepper
- 1 Celery stalk
- ⅓ Lemon
- Small piece of red Chili Pepper
- ½ Garlic clove

Directions

- Cut the red bell pepper into 4 pieces. Remove the seeds. Cut it into smaller pieces
- Cut the celery stalk into pieces of 1 - 1.5 inches (2 - 3 cm)
- Peel the lemon, cut out a 1/3 part and put the rest away
- Cut the chili pepper in half. Remove the seeds
- Turn on the juicer
- Put the red bell pepper, celery stalk, lemon, red chili pepper and garlic clove in the juicer, piece by piece
- End with a piece of red bell pepper
- Pour into a glass, serve and drink immediately

***

4. Veggie Cocktail

This is a popular recipe to increase alertness and energy. It is packed with nutrients, yet very low in calories.

Ingredients

- ½ Beetroot
- 1 Carrot
- 1 Celery Stalk
- ½ Cucumber

Directions

- Cut the beetroot in half
- Cut the carrot lengthwise. Then slice it into parts about the size of thick potato fries
- Cut the leaves of the celery into big pieces. Then cut the stalk lengthwise, into pieces of 0.5 - 1 inches (1 - 2 cm)
- Cut the cucumber lengthwise
- Turn on the juicer
- Put the beetroot, carrot, celery and cucumber in the juicer, piece by piece. The power of the juicer will pull the cucumber in automatically
- End with a piece of carrot
- Pour into a glass, serve and drink immediately

***

5. Mint Refreshment

This delicious green juice is not only very tasty, but also refreshing: you will feel rejuvenated afterwards!

Ingredients

- ⅓ Cucumber
- 1 Green Apple
- 1 Pear
- 4 fresh Mint leaves
- 1 handful of Parsley

Directions

- Cut the cucumber lengthwise
- Cut the apple into 6 pieces
- Cut the pear into 6 pieces
- Turn on the juicer
- Put the cucumber, green apple, pear, mint leaves and parsley in the juicer, piece by piece
- End with a piece of apple
- Pour into a glass, serve and drink immediately

***

6. Digestion Booster

This is a fantastic juice if you have digestive problems.

Ingredients

- Handful of Watercress
- 2 Broccoli Stalks
- 1 Celery Stalk
- ½ Pineapple

Directions

- Cut the watercress into big pieces. The stems give off a lot of flavor and juice
- Cut the broccoli into pieces of about 1 - 1.5 inches (2 - 3 cm)
- Cut the celery lengthwise into pieces of 1 - 1.5 inches (2 - 3 cm)
- Peel the pineapple
- Cut the pineapple in long pieces, and then into smaller pieces of 0.5 - 1 inches (1 - 2 cm)
- Turn on the juicer
- Put the watercress, broccoli, celery and pineapple in the juicer, piece by piece
- Pour into a glass, serve and drink immediately

***

7. Kiwi Attack

Kiwis are not only high in Vitamin C, but also help induce sleep and improve digestion.

Ingredients

- ¼ Pineapple
- 2 Kiwis
- 1 Celery stalk
- 1 Lemon slice (with peel)

Directions

- Remove the peel of the pineapple. Cut the pineapple into long slices, and then into smaller pieces of 0.5 - 1 inches (1 - 2 cm)
- Cut the top of the kiwis. Peel them. Cut them into 4 parts
- Cut the celery lengthwise into pieces of 1 - 1.5 inches (2 - 3 cm)
- Turn on the juicer
- Put the pineapple, kiwis, celery and lemon slice in the juicer, piece by piece
- Pour into a glass, serve and drink immediately

***

8. Thirst Quencher

This juice is perfect for a hot day. Drink this, and you won't be thirsty anymore!

Ingredients

- ½ Cucumber
- 1 Celery stalk
- 2 Basil twigs
- 2 Tomatoes

Directions

- Cut the cucumber lengthwise
- Cut the celery stalk into pieces of 1 - 1.5 inches (2 - 3 cm)
- Cut each tomato into 4 parts
- Turn on the juicer
- Put the cucumber, celery, tomato and basil in the juicer, piece by piece
- End with a piece of cucumber
- Pour into a glass, serve and drink immediately

***

9. Rhubarb and Mint

Rhubarb is considered a fruit in the US, although most countries consider it a vegetable. Perhaps a case of 'You say to-may-to, I say to-mah-to'. Regardless, rhubarb is associated with many health benefits, such as improving digestion, stimulating bone growth, and preventing Alzheimer's disease.

Ingredients

- 3 Rhubarb Stalks
- 1 Mint twig

Directions

- Cut each rhubarb stalk into pieces of 1 - 1.5 inches (2 - 3 cm)
- Turn on the juicer
- Put the rhubarb and mint in the juicer, piece by piece
- Pour into a glass, serve and drink immediately

***

10. Carrot and Bell Pepper

Another juice with two of the top 10 recommended vegetables. And so tasty!

Ingredients

- 1 Carrot
- 2 Orange Bell Peppers
- 1 Lemon Slice (without peel)

Directions

- Cut the carrot lengthwise. Then slice it into parts about the size of thick potato fries
- Cut the bell peppers into 4 parts. Remove the seeds. Then cut them into smaller pieces
- Turn on the juicer
- Put the carrot, bell peppers and lemon in the juicer, piece by piece
- End with a piece of carrot
- Pour into a glass, serve and drink immediately

***

11. V8-copycat

To deliver a peak performance, a sports car needs the best possible fuel. So does your body. This drink will energize you for the whole day!

Ingredients

- 2 Carrots
- ½ Beetroot
- 1 Celery stalk
- 1 Parsley twig
- 3 Tomatoes
- ¼ white onion
- Handful fresh Spinach
- 1 Garlic clove

Directions

- Cut the carrot lengthwise. Then slice it into parts about the size of thick potato fries
- Cut the beetroot in half. Put one half away. Cut the other half into pieces of 0.5 - 1 inches (1 - 2 cm)
- Cut the celery lengthwise into pieces of 1 inch (2 cm)
- Cut the parsley twig into 3 parts
- Cut the tomatoes in half
- Cut the onion into big pieces of 1 - 1.5 inches (2 - 3 cm)
- Turn on the juicer
- Put the carrots, beetroot, celery, parsley, tomatoes, onion, spinach and garlic in the juicer, piece by piece

- Use the pusher to make sure all the spinach leaves are juiced
- End with a piece of carrot
- Pour into a glass, serve and drink immediately

***

12. Yellow Tomato Juice

Because of the added lemongrass, this delicious tomato juice has a unique taste.

Ingredients

- 1 Apple
- 1 Lemongrass stalk
- Handful Yellow Cherry Tomatoes
- 2 Basil leaves

Directions

- Cut the apple into 6 pieces
- Cut the lemongrass stalk into pieces of 1 - 1.5 inches (2 - 3 cm)
- Turn on the juicer
- Put the apple, lemongrass, cherry tomatoes and basil in the juicer, piece by piece
- Pour into a glass, serve and drink immediately

***

13. Gazpacho Twist

A juicer can also be used to make all kinds of soups. This recipe is a twist on the classic Spanish Gazpacho, which is a cold tomato soup. But for this recipe we will use cucumber instead of tomatoes. Try it out and see if you like it!

Ingredients

- 1 Cucumber
- 2 Basil leaves
- 1 Garlic clove
- A few drops of Tabasco (to taste)
- A pinch of Sea Salt

Directions

- Cut the cucumber lengthwise
- Turn on the juicer
- Put the cucumber, basil and garlic in the juicer, piece by piece
- Add tabasco and sea salt
- End with a piece of cucumber
- Pour into a glass, serve and drink immediately

***

14. Tropical Surprise

This delicious juice gets you in the summer mood!

Ingredients

- 1 Pear
- ⅓ Pineapple
- ⅓ Lime with peel

Directions

- Peel the pear. Remove the core. Cut it into slices of 0.5 inches (1 cm)
- Remove the peel of the pineapple. Cut the pineapple into long slices, and then into smaller pieces of 0.5 - 1 inches (1 - 2 cm)
- Cut the lime into small slices
- Turn on the juicer
- Put the pear, pineapple and lime in the juicer, piece by piece
- Pour into a glass, serve and drink immediately

***

9. Juicing Recipes - Summer

The sun shines, everyone's wearing shorts or skirts, people are smiling: Summer is here!

In this chapter, you will find delicious recipes for summer juices.

The names of the recipes are:

- Melon Beauty
- Green Surprise
- Kinky Drink
- Get In Shape
- Sweet Fennel
- Creamy Melon
- Pineapple and Mango
- Tanned Skin
- Livestrong Melon
- Chili
- Beetroot & Dill
- Heaven in a Glass
- Pak Choi

Let's begin with the Melon Beauty juice!

***

15. Melon Beauty

This juice not only tastes phenomenal, it is also very refreshing and thirst quenching, because cucumber and melon both contain a lot of water.

Ingredients

- ¼ Cucumber
- ¼ Melon (any kind; yellow melons taste sweeter than watermelon because they contain more sugars)
- 1 Pear
- 2 Mint leaves

Directions

- Cut the cucumber lengthwise
- Cut out 1/4th of the melon. Then place that piece of melon on its flat side on a cutting board. This way you prevent cutting yourself. Peel the lemon and cut it into pieces of 1.5- 2 inches (4 - 5 cm)
- Peel the pear. Remove the core. Cut it into slices of 0.5 inches (1 cm).
- Turn on the juicer
- First put the mint leaves in the juicer
- Then put in the cucumber, melon and pear, piece by piece
- End with a piece of cucumber
- Pour into a glass, serve and drink immediately

***

16. Green Surprise

Broccoli is an excellent source of Vitamin C and Vitamin K. It helps reduce bad cholesterol, decreases inflammation, and is good for your heart.

Ingredients

- 6 Broccoli stalks
- 1 Pear
- 2 Celery stalks

Directions

- Cut the broccoli into pieces of about 1.5 inches (3 - 4 cm)
- Peel the pear. Remove the core. Cut it into slices of 0.5 inches (1 cm).
- Cut the celery into pieces of 1 - 1.5 inches (2 - 3 cm)
- Turn on the juicer
- Put the broccoli, pear and celery in the juicer, piece by piece
- Pour into a glass, serve and drink immediately

***

17. Kinky Drink

Linseed is a great vegetarian source of Alpha-Linolenic Acid (ALA), an Omega 3 essential fatty acid. It reduces inflammation and promotes good bowel movements. Linseed and blackberries also improve skin quality. This juice is a real winner!

Ingredients

- 1 Apple
- 1 Celery stalk
- 4.5 oz (125 gr.) Blackberries
- ½ inch (1 cm) Ginger Root
- 1 ts Linseed Oil

Directions

- Remove the core from the apple. Cut it into 6 pieces
- Cut the celery stalk into pieces of 1 - 1.5 inches (2 - 3 cm)
- Turn on the juicer
- Put the apple, celery, blackberries and ginger root in the juicer, piece by piece
- End with a piece of apple
- Pour into a glass. Add the linseed oil. Serve and drink immediately

***

18. Get In Shape

Blue grapes contain powerful antioxidants, making your immune system stronger. They also help relieve chronic constipation.

Ingredients

- ¼ Watermelon
- 7 oz. (200 gr.) Blue Grapes
- 1 Lemon slice (without peel)

Directions

- Cut out 1/4th of the melon. Then place that piece of melon on its flat side on a cutting board. This way you prevent cutting yourself. Peel the lemon, and cut it into pieces of 1.5- 2 inches (4 - 5 cm)
- Turn on the juicer
- Put the watermelon, blue grapes and lemon in the juicer, piece by piece
- Pour into a glass, serve and drink immediately

***

19. Sweet Fennel

Fennel is a great source of potassium, which helps reduce blood pressure. It also tastes great, it has a mild licorice flavor. Try it for yourself!

Ingredients

- ⅓ Pineapple
- 1 Green Apple
- 1 small Fennel

Directions

- Remove the peel of the pineapple. Cut out 1/3th of the fruit, put the rest away. Cut the pineapple into long slices, and then into smaller pieces of 0.5 - 1 inches (1 - 2 cm)
- Remove the core from the apple. Cut it into 6 pieces
- Cut the fennel in half, and then into pieces of about 1 - 1.5 inches (2 - 3 cm)
- Turn on the juicer
- Put the pineapple, apple and fennel in the juicer, piece by piece
- Pour into a glass, serve and drink immediately

***

20. Creamy Melon

Pears are rich in water-soluble fibers like pectin. Avocado is one of the best sources of mono-unsaturated fatty acids. Combined in a juice, this mixture helps the basal metabolic rate, and has a very good tonifying effect on the bowel.

Ingredients

- 1 Pear
- 2 Cantaloupe or Galia Melon slices
- ½ Avocado
- A couple of fresh Mint leaves

Directions

- Peel the pear. Remove the core. Cut it into slices of 0.5 inches (1 cm)
- Cut out two big slices from the melon, put the rest away. Peel the melon. Cut it into 4 pieces
- Cut the avocado in two, remove the pit. Put one half away. Remove the peel of the other half. Cut it into 4 pieces
- Turn on the juicer
- Put the pear, melon, avocado and mint leaves in the juicer, piece by piece. You will find that the avocado will be completely absorbed by the structure of the pear and melon
- End with a piece of melon
- Pour into a glass, serve and drink immediately

***

21. Pineapple and Mango

The perfect drink for a hot summer day!

Ingredients

- ⅓ Pineapple
- 1 Mango (ripe)
- ½ Rosemary twig

Directions

- Remove the peel of the pineapple. Cut the pineapple into long slices, and then into smaller pieces of 0.5 - 1 inches (1 - 2 cm)
- Cut the mango in half. Remove the pit. Take out the fruit with a spoon. Cut it into smaller pieces
- Turn on the juicer
- Put the pineapple, mango and rosemary in the juicer, piece by piece
- Pour into a glass, serve and drink immediately

***

22. Tanned Skin

Who doesn't want to have the perfect beach body? Carrots and mangos are rich in beta-Carotene, which protects your skin from getting sunburned, and instead helps you get tanned more easily.

Ingredients

- 2 Carrots
- ½ Mango (with peel)
- ½ inch (1 cm) Ginger Root

Directions

- Cut the carrot lengthwise. Then slice it into parts about the size of thick potato fries
- Cut the mango into smaller pieces
- Turn on the juicer
- Put the carrots, mango and ginger root in the juicer, piece by piece
- End with a piece of carrot
- Pour into a glass, serve and drink immediately

***

23. Livestrong Melon

This juice is almost like natural doping, you will immediately feel a surge of energy rushing through your body!

Ingredients

- ½ Watermelon or Galia Melon
- ⅓ Lemon
- 1 Lemongrass stalk
- 1 Parsley or Mint twig

Directions

- Cut the melon in half. Put one half away in the fridge for later use. Place the other half on its flat side on a cutting board. This way you prevent cutting yourself. Peel the lemon, and cut it into pieces of 1.5- 2 inches (4 - 5 cm)
- Cut out one-third of the lemon, put the rest away. Peel the lemon. Cut it into half.
- Cut the lemongrass stalk into pieces of 0.5 inches (1 cm)
- Turn on the juicer
- Put the melon, lemon and lemongrass in the juicer, piece by piece
- Pour into a glass, serve with the parsley/mint twig and drink immediately

***

24. Chili

Tomato juice with a spicy twist. Tomatoes are a major source of lycopene, an antioxidant that helps reduce risk of heart disease and certain types of cancer.

Ingredients

- 4 Tomatoes
- 1 Celery stalk
- ½ red Chili Pepper

Directions

- Cut the tomatoes into 4 parts
- Cut the celery stalk into pieces of 1 - 1.5 inches (2 - 3 cm)
- Cut the chili pepper in half. Remove the seeds.
- Turn on the juicer
- Put the tomatoes, celery and chili pepper in the juicer, piece by piece
- Pour into a glass, serve and drink immediately

***

25. Beetroot & Dill

Beetroot is one of the top 10 recommended vegetables. This superfood boosts your immune system and is great for detoxification. And this juice tastes really good too, because of the added banana!

Ingredients

- 2 Beetroots
- 1 Lemon slice
- 1 Banana
- 1 Dill twig

Directions

- Cut the beetroot in half, and then into pieces of 0.5 - 1 inches (1 - 2 cm)
- Peel the lemon slice
- Peel the banana. Cut it into pieces
- Turn on the juicer
- Put the beetroot, lemon, banana and dill in the juicer, piece by piece. This way, the structure of the beetroot will mix best with the juice and flavor of the banana
- Pour into a glass, serve and drink immediately

***

26. Heaven In A Glass

The taste of this juice may be the closest thing to reaching heaven on earth.

Ingredients

- ½ Mango
- 1 Grapefruit
- 3.5 oz (100 gr.) Raspberries
- 1 Lime slice (with peel)

Directions

- Cut the mango in half. Remove the pit. Put one half away. Use a spoon to take out the fruit of the other half. Cut it into smaller pieces
- Remove the peel of the grapefruit. Cut it into 4 parts
- Turn on the juicer
- Put the mango, grapefruit, raspberries and lime in the juicer, piece by piece
- Pour into a glass, serve and drink immediately

***

27. Pak Choi

Pak choi, also called bok choy, is a Chinese cabbage with smooth, dark green leaf blades. It is high in Vitamin C, which works as an antioxidant in the body and protects your cells. Pak choi also helps in growing stronger bones.

Ingredients

- ½ Fennel Bulb
- 1 Celery stalk
- 1 Lemon slice (without peel)
- A couple of Pak Choi leaves

Directions

- Cut the fennel in half, and then into pieces of about 1 - 1.5 inches (2 - 3 cm)
- Cut the celery stalk into pieces of 1 - 1.5 inches (2 - 3 cm)
- Cut the pak choi into strips
- Turn on the juicer
- Put the fennel, celery, lemon and pak choi in the juicer, piece by piece
- Use the pusher when putting in the pak choi
- Pour into a glass, serve and drink immediately

10. Juicing Recipes - Autumn

Summer has passed, and it's starting to get a little chilly. Different times, different juices.

In this chapter, you will find recipes for juices that taste best in autumn.

The names of the recipes are:

- Sweet Potato & Rosemary
- Pear & Celery
- Rose Bowl
- Spicy Carrot
- Pear & Grape
- Pumpkin & Orange
- Pear & Spinach
- Chinese Cabbage & Pineapple
- Green Desire
- Berry Madness
- Ecstasy Forever
- Apple Softener

Let's begin with the Sweet Potato & Rosemary juice!

***

28. Sweet Potato & Rosemary

Yes, you can juice sweet potatoes! Because they are not a fruit, but a part of the starch family, they give a slightly thicker consistency to your juice and add their unique sweetness to it.

Ingredients

- ½ Sweet Potato (with peel)
- 3 Carrots
- ½ Rosemary twig
- Pinch of Cinnamon Powder

Directions

- Cut the sweet potato in two. Put one half away. Cut the other half into pieces of 1 - 1.5 inches (2 - 3 cm)
- Cut the carrot lengthwise. Then slice it into parts about the size of thick potato fries
- Cut the rosemary twig into 4 small pieces
- Turn on the juicer
- Put the sweet potato, carrot and rosemary in the juicer, piece by piece
- End with a piece of carrot
- Pour into a glass and add a pinch of cinnamon. Serve and drink immediately

***

29. Pear & Celery

If you have little time, this is a quick and easy healthy green juice to make.

Ingredients

- 1 big Pear (with peel)
- 2 Celery stalks

Directions

- Remove the core of the pear. Cut it into slices of 0.5 inches (1 cm)
- Cut the celery stalk into pieces of 1 - 1.5 inches (2 - 3 cm)
- Turn on the juicer
- Put the pear and celery in the juicer, piece by piece
- Pour into a glass, serve and drink immediately

***

30. Rose Bowl

Cranberries have amazing health benefits. They can help relieve respiratory disorders and kidney stones. Also, they prevent stomach disorders and promote good heart health. Mix in the celery and ginger, and you have an insanely powerful drink!

Ingredients

- 1 Celery stalk
- 1 Apple
- ½ inch (1 cm) Ginger Root
- Handful of Cranberries
- 2-3 Mint leaves

Directions

- Cut the celery stalk into pieces of 1 - 1.5 inches (2 - 3 cm)
- Remove the core from the apple. Cut it into 6 pieces
- Turn on the juicer
- Put the celery, apple, ginger, cranberries and mint in the juicer, piece by piece
- End with a piece of apple
- Pour into a glass, serve and drink immediately

***

31. Spicy Carrot

This tasty juice walks a fine line between sweetness and spiciness. Luckily, the lemongrass takes off the rough edges, making drinking this carrot juice a blissful experience.

Ingredients

- 4 Carrots
- 1 orange or red Chili Pepper
- ½ Lemongrass stalk

Directions

- Cut the carrots lengthwise. Then slice it into parts about the size of thick potato fries
- Cut the chili pepper in half. Remove the seeds
- Cut the lemongrass stalk in half. Put one half away. Cut the other half into pieces of about 0.5 - 1 inches (1 - 2 cm)
- Turn on the juicer
- Put the carrot, chili pepper and lemon grass in the juicer, piece by piece
- End with a piece of carrot
- Pour into a glass, serve and drink immediately

***

32. Pear & Grape

This is a great drink when you crave a glass of white wine, but hesitate because that little voice in the back of your mind tells you to drink a healthy juice instead.

Ingredients

- 1 ripe Pear (with peel)
- 15-20 White Grapes

Directions

- Remove the core of the pear. Cut it into 4 parts
- Turn on the juicer
- Put the pear and white grapes in the juicer, piece by piece
- Pour into a glass, serve and drink immediately

***

33. Pumpkin & Orange

Pumpkins are rich in carotenoids, just like carrots. These promote good eye health, improve skin health and can even help prevent certain types of cancer.

Ingredients

- 1 Pumpkin slice
- 2 Oranges

Directions

- Peel the pumpkin. Cut the pumpkin slice into pieces of 1.5 inches (3-4 cm)
- Peel the orange. Cut it into 4 parts
- Turn on the juicer
- Put the pumpkin and oranges in the juicer, piece by piece
- Pour into a glass, serve and drink immediately

***

34. Pear & Spinach

Has someone ever told you: "When you are green inside, you are clean inside"? This isn't to be taken literally of course, but refers to the many health benefits of green produce. And spinach is one of the healthiest green vegetables out there.

Ingredients

- 1 big juicy Pear
- 3 hands full of Spinach

Directions

- Peel the pear. Remove the core. Cut it into slices of 0.5 inches (1 cm)
- Cut the spinach into big chunks
- Turn on the juicer
- Put the pear and spinach in the juicer, piece by piece
- Use the pusher for the spinach
- End with a piece of pear
- Pour into a glass, serve and drink immediately

***

35. Chinese Cabbage & Pineapple

Do you suffer from stomach ulcers? Then you should drink this juice. Cabbage contains gefarnate and L-glutamine, which protect the mucous-membrane lining of your stomach.

Ingredients

- 1 Corncob
- ⅓ Pineapple
- 2 - 3 Chinese Cabbage leaves

Directions

- Cut the cob in half. Place it vertically on a cutting board. Use a sharp kitchen knife to cut the corn of the cob.
- Remove the peel of the pineapple. Cut out 1/3rd of the fruit, put the rest away. Cut the pineapple into long slices, and then into smaller pieces of 0.5 - 1 inches (1 - 2 cm)
- Cut the Chinese cabbage leaves in half
- Turn on the juicer
- Put the corn, pineapple and Chinese cabbage in the juicer, piece by piece
- Pour into a glass, serve and drink immediately

***

36. Green Desire

This is as good as apple juice can get! The ginger adds a little bit of a bite, while the lime and mint keep it fresh. The mint in this juice also has a soothing effect on your intestines.

Ingredients

- 2 green Apples
- ½ inch (1 cm) Ginger Root
- A couple of Mint leaves
- ½ Lime (with peel)

Directions

- Remove the core from the apple. Cut it into 6 pieces
- Cut the lime in two. Put one half away. Cut the other half into 4 parts
- Turn on the juicer
- Put the apples, ginger, mint and lime in the juicer, piece by piece
- End with a piece of apple
- Pour into a glass, serve and drink immediately

***

37. Berry Madness

This recipe is one of my favorites. Berries have incredible health benefits. Every body tissue and function is positively impacted by the flavonoids in them. And this fun juice tastes and looks great too! If you want to convince someone else to start juicing, make them this drink.

Ingredients

- 1 Apple
- 4.5 oz (125 gr.) Blackberries
- 4.5 oz (125 gr.) Blueberries
- 1.7 oz (50 gr.) Cranberries

Directions

- Remove the core from the apple. Cut it into 6 pieces
- Turn on the juicer
- Put the apple, blackberries, blueberries and cranberries in the juicer, piece by piece
- Pour into a glass, serve and drink immediately

***

38. Ecstasy Forever

This juice is a great way to start the day, especially if you are on a juice fast. It is jam-packed with healthy nutrients like Vitamin C, iron, pectin and antioxidants. This juice helps to burn fat, get rid of toxins and improves digestion.

Ingredients

- 1 Apple
- ⅓ Lemon
- ½ Fennel
- 1 Pear
- ⅓ Parsnip
- Handful of Grapes
- A few Mint or Basil leaves

Directions

- Remove the core from the apple. Cut it into 6 pieces
- Cut the fennel in half. Put one half away. Cut the other half into pieces of about 1 - 1.5 inches (2 - 3 cm)
- Remove the core of the pear. Cut it into slices of 0.5 inches (1 cm)
- Cut off ⅓ of the parsnip. Put the rest away. Cut the parsnip into pieces of about 1 - 1.5 inches (2 - 3 cm)
- Turn on the juicer. Put the apple, lemon, fennel, pear, parsnip, grapes and mint/basil leaves in the juicer, piece by piece. End with a piece of apple
- Pour into a glass, serve and drink immediately

***

39. Apple Softener

The apple, carrot and celery in this juice mix really well together, while the fennel adds a gentle licorice flavor.

Ingredients

- 1 green Apple
- 1 Carrot
- 1 Celery stalk
- ⅓ Fennel bulb

Directions

- Remove the core from the apple. Cut it into 6 pieces
- Cut the carrot lengthwise. Then slice it into parts about the size of thick potato fries
- Cut the celery stalk into pieces of 1 - 1.5 inches (2 - 3 cm)
- Cut the fennel in half, and then into pieces of about 1 - 1.5 inches (2 - 3 cm)
- Turn on the juicer
- Put the apple, carrot, celery and fennel in the juicer, piece by piece
- End with a piece of apple
- Pour into a glass, serve and drink immediately

***

11. Juicing Recipes - Winter

Winter has come. It's cold outside! Let's see if we can bring a little warmth to our lives with these winter juices.

The names of the recipes in this final chapter:

- Hulk Cappuccino
- Pretty Prozac
- Walnut Juice
- Pumpkin & Parsnip
- Mineral Shot
- Anti-Flu
- Digestion Fantasy
- Health Shot
- Winter Vibes
- White Cabbage
- Pampering

Let's begin with the Hulk Cappuccino juice!

***

40. Hulk Cappuccino

The Hulk is super strong AND green. Coincidence? I think not. This creamy green juice gives you an immediate power boost!

Ingredients

- Big Kale leaf
- 2 Apples
- ¼ Fennel
- 1 Lemon slice (without peel)

Directions

- Cut the kale into pieces of 1 - 1.5 inches (2 - 3 cm)
- Remove the core from the apples. Cut it into 6 pieces
- Cut out ¼th of the fennel. Put the rest away. Cut the fennel into pieces of about 1 - 1.5 inches (2 - 3 cm)
- Turn on the juicer
- Put the kale, apple, fennel and lemon slice in the juicer, piece by piece
- Pour into a glass, serve and drink immediately

***

41. Pretty Prozac

Ever suffer from winter depression? Although it is not the real thing, this nomnomnom juice will bring just that little bit of sunshine and warmth to your day that you are missing so dearly!

Ingredients

- 1 Winter Carrot
- 1 Apple
- ½ Fennel
- 1 Lemongrass stalk

Directions

- Cut the winter carrot lengthwise. Then slice it into parts about the size of thick potato fries
- Remove the core from the apple. Cut it into 6 pieces
- Cut the fennel in half. Put one half away. Cut the fennel into pieces of about 1 - 1.5 inches (2 - 3 cm)
- Cut the lemongrass stalk into pieces of about 0.5 - 1 inches (1 - 2 cm)
- Turn on the juicer
- Put the winter carrot, apple, fennel and lemongrass in the juicer, piece by piece
- Pour into a glass, serve and drink immediately

***

42. Walnut Juice

This healthy green juice is surprisingly rich in taste. And with the added walnuts, this juice wouldn't look out of place on the menu of a fancy restaurant!

Ingredients

- 2 green Apples
- 1 Celery stalk
- Handful of Parsley
- ⅓ Lime (with peel)
- 5 Walnuts

Directions

- Remove the core from the apples. Cut it into 6 pieces
- Cut the celery stalk into pieces of 1 - 1.5 inches (2 - 3 cm)
- Cut the parsley into smaller pieces
- Cut out ⅓rd of the lime. Put the rest away. Cut the lime part into 3 slices
- Turn on the juicer
- Put the apples, celery, parsley and lime in the juicer, piece by piece
- Pour into a glass. Serve with the walnuts on the side (do not put them in the juicer).
- Drink immediately

***

43. Pumpkin & Parsnip

Parsnips and carrots belong to the same family, but parsnip juice contains a lot less calories than carrot juice. This makes parsnip an excellent ingredient if you are juicing to lose weight.

Ingredients

- 1 Pumpkin slice
- ½ Parsnip
- ⅓ Lemon
- 1 Celery stalk

Directions

- Peel the pumpkin. Cut the pumpkin slice into pieces of 1.5 inches (3 - 4 cm)
- Cut the parsnip in half. Put one half away. Cut the parsnip into pieces of about 1 - 1.5 inches (2 - 3 cm)
- Cut out ⅓rd of the lemon. Put the rest away. Peel the lemon.
- Cut the celery stalk into pieces of 1 - 1.5 inches (2 - 3 cm)
- Turn on the juicer
- Put the pumpkin, parsnip, lemon and celery in the juicer, piece by piece
- Pour into a glass, serve and drink immediately

***

44. Mineral Shot

This mineral shot is a spectacular immune system fortifier. Kale is rich in vitamins K, A and C. It not only helps lower bad cholesterol, but also supports cardiovascular health. Add a carrot, some parsley and a little bit of lime, and you have the perfect detox juice.

Ingredients

- 7 oz (200 gr.) Kale
- 1 Carrot
- Handful of Parsley
- ⅓ Lime (with peel)

Directions

- Cut the kale into pieces of 1 - 1.5 inches (2 - 3 cm)
- Cut the carrot lengthwise. Then slice it into parts about the size of thick potato fries
- Cut out ⅓ of the lime. Put the rest away.
- Turn on the juicer
- Put the kale, carrot, parsley and lime in the juicer, piece by piece
- Pour into a glass, serve and drink immediately

***

45. Anti-Flu

This is an excellent juice to drink when you have the flu, or feel a cold coming on. Take a sip, relax and let this juice do its magic!

Ingredients

- 1 Carrot
- 1 green Apple
- 1 Lime
- 2 Kiwis

Directions

- Cut the carrot lengthwise. Then slice it into parts about the size of thick potato fries
- Remove the core from the apple. Cut it into 6 parts
- Peel the lime. Cut it into 4 parts
- Cut the top of the kiwis. Peel them. Cut them into 4 parts
- Turn on the juicer
- Put the carrot, apple, lime and kiwis in the juicer, piece by piece
- Pour into a glass, serve and drink immediately

***

46. Digestion Fantasy

Most kids don't like to eat their greens. Drinking them though is something else. This is a green juice that is so fresh and delicious that your kids will love it!

Ingredients

- 2 big White Cabbage leaves
- ⅓ Pineapple
- 5 Mint leaves
- ½ inch (1 cm) Ginger Root

Directions

- Cut the white cabbage into pieces of 1 - 1.5 inches (2 - 3 cm)
- Remove the peel of the pineapple. Cut out ⅓rd of the fruit, put the rest away. Cut the pineapple into long slices, and then into smaller pieces of 0.5 - 1 inches (1 - 2 cm)
- Turn on the juicer
- Put the white cabbage, pineapple, mint and ginger root in the juicer, piece by piece
- Pour into a glass, serve and drink immediately

***

47. Health Shot

This is an incredible drink if you are feeling somewhat down and out. The leafy greens of chicory and pak choi, combined with celery, are like a nitro boost to your natural defense system.

Ingredients

- 1 Celery stalk
- 1 small Chicory
- 1 big Pak Choi leaf
- 2 Lemon slices

Directions

- Cut the celery stalk into pieces of 1 - 1.5 inches (2 - 3 cm)
- Cut the chicory lengthwise into 4 parts
- Cut the pak choi into pieces of 1 - 1.5 inches (2 - 3 cm)
- Turn on the juicer
- Put the celery, chicory, pak choi and lemon in the juicer, piece by piece
- Pour into a glass, serve and drink immediately

***

48. Winter Vibes

This juice is a super breakfast. It is stuffed with enzymes, making this an incredible way to start the day.

Ingredients

- 3 Kiwis
- 1 Apple
- 1 Lemon (without peel)
- ½ inch (1 cm) Ginger Root
- A little bit of Cardamom

Directions

- Cut the top of the kiwis. Peel them. Cut the kiwis into 4 parts
- Remove the core from the apple. Cut it into 6 pieces
- Peel the lemon. Cut it into 4 parts
- Turn on the juicer
- Put the kiwi, apple, lemon, ginger root and cardamom in the juicer, piece by piece
- End with a piece of apple
- Pour into a glass, serve and drink immediately

***

49. White Cabbage

White cabbage is one of those power veggies. It helps the brain and nervous system to function properly, reduces arthritis pain and inflammation, and strengthens the bones. White cabbage is slightly bitter in taste, but this is balanced by the anise, licorice flavor of the fennel.

Ingredients

- 2 big White Cabbage leaves
- ½ Fennel
- Lemon slice (without peel)

Directions

- Cu the white cabbage leaves into pieces of 1 - 1.5 inches (2 - 3 cm)
- Cut the fennel in half. Put one half away. Cut the other half into pieces of about 1 - 1.5 inches (2 - 3 cm)
- Turn on the juicer
- Put the white cabbage, fennel and lemon slice in the juicer, piece by piece
- Pour into a glass, serve and drink immediately

***

50. Pampering

This tea is the perfect drink if you feel like giving yourself a treat. Moreover, it is also really good for you when you feel a bit cold. It will warm you up from the inside and help you sweat out toxins.

Ingredients

- 1.2 inches (3 cm) Turmeric (with peel)
- 1.2 inches (3 cm) Ginger Root (with peel)
- 1 Lemongrass stalk
- Boiling Water
- Honey

Directions

- Cut the turmeric into small slices
- Cut the ginger root into small slices
- Cut the lemongrass stalk into pieces of about 0.5 - 1 inches (1 - 2 cm)
- Turn on the juicer
- Put the turmeric, ginger and lemongrass in the juicer, piece by piece
- Pour into a glass. Pour the boiling water on top. Add some honey. Serve, but don't burn your tongue: don't drink the juice when it is still too hot.

***

12. Free Resources

If you would like to learn more about juicing, here are some great free resources to get you started.

***

Documentaries

These documentaries can all be watched for free on Youtube:

- **Fat, Sick and Nearly Dead:** follow Joe Cross on his 60-day juice fast while traveling the United States.
- **Fat, Sick and Nearly Dead 2:** the sequel to the movie that inspired so many to start juicing.
- **Super Juice Me:** see what happens when Jason Vale, a nr. 1 best-selling health author, invites 8 people with a total of 22 different health conditions to join him on a 28-day juice fast.
- **The Joy of Juicing:** this documentary does not only cover juicing. Rather, it takes a holistic approach at our health through diet, exercise, stress management and detoxification.
- **Dying to Have Known:** another documentary that focuses on an alternative approach to health: Gerson Therapy. This is a natural treatment that activates the body's amazing ability to heal itself through a plant-based diet, which includes juicing.

***

Websites

- **Rebootwithjoe.com:** Joe Cross's website, of Fat, Sick and Nearly Dead fame.
- **Fitlive.tv:** Join Drew Canole and the Fitlife community to take back control of your health and change your life.
- **Discountjuicers.com:** looks like a website that was designed in the 90s, but looks can be deceiving. This website contains a ton of valuable info about the different types of juicers on the market.
- **All-about-juicing.com:** Lots of info on juicers and juicing here.

***

Youtube channels

- **Fat, Sick and Nearly Dead**
- **Fitlive.tv**
- **Official Juice Plus**
- **Discount Juicers**

Conclusion

Thank you for reading this book, *'Juicing For Beginners: Feel Great Again With These 50 Weight Loss Juice Recipes!'*

I hope you have learned a lot about juicing, and feel comfortable – and excited! – to start juicing and experience the many health benefits yourself.

By reading this book you have learned:

- The Basics of Juicing
- The Health Benefits of Juicing
- The Difference Between Juicing and Blending
- What to Look for When Buying a Juicer
- How to Make a Juice
- The Top 10 Best Vegetables to Juice
- How to do a Juice Fast, and
- 50 Juicing Recipes to get you started!

The next step is to apply what you have learned and start juicing regularly. This can be a challenging process at times. We all have our moments of weakness, and cookies or deep-fried chicken are often much more tempting than a healthy juice. Take it one step at a time. And don't beat yourself up if you temporarily fall off track. Nobody is perfect! Success is simply a matter of getting up one more time than you fall.

I wish you success on your juicing journey, and I hope you quickly start reaping the amazing health benefits that juicing has to offer.

***

Finally, if you enjoyed this book, I would like to ask you for a favor. Would you be kind enough to share your thoughts and post a review of this book on Amazon? You can search for it on Amazon, or go to:

bit.ly/juicingreview

Your voice is important for this book to reach as many people as possible. The more reviews this book gets, the more people will be able to find it and enjoy the incredible health benefits of juicing.

Thank you again for buying this book and good luck with juicing!

BONUS CHAPTER: What is Intermittent Fasting

I hope you enjoyed this book *'Juicing For Beginners'*. If you did, you may also be interested in my other book: *'Intermittent Fasting: Burn Fat, Lose Weight And Build Muscle With Ease While Still Eating Your Favorite Foods!'*

What follows is the first chapter from that book!

***

"I feel so much better on it. I haven't put on nearly the amount of fat I normally would. And the great thing about this diet is, I sleep so much better."

Hugh Jackman, of Wolverine fame, on how intermittent fasting helps him bulk and cut for movie roles.

Key Takeaway: Intermittent Fasting is a form of dieting where one alternates between periods of absolute fasting and eating. This form of fasting has many health benefits. Also, it doesn't place any constraints on what you have to eat and what you don't.

Intermittent fasting seems to be the recent fad that has taken over the world of fitness trends. Intermittent fasting involves oscillating between periods of fasting and eating. There are studies that show that this diet can indeed facilitate weight loss, improve immunity, and promote your metabolism as well. In this chapter, you will learn what intermittent fasting is all about.

***

Intermittent Fasting 101

Intermittent fasting is about alternating between periods of eating and fasting. The focus isn't so much on the kind of foods you should consume; instead, the focus is on when you should eat.

You might have never thought of it, but everyone fasts every day. When you are getting your ZZZs! Think of intermittent fasting as a simple extension of that fasting period.

There are different methods of intermittent fasting. The 16:8 method is perhaps the most common one. With this method, you are fasting for about 16 hours in a day. Your eating window is restricted to an 8-hour cycle. For example, you skip your breakfast; have your first meal at noon and the last one at 8pm. Later on in this book, we will discuss the most popular intermittent fasting methods.

Notwithstanding what people usually assume, intermittent fasting is relatively easy to follow. Hunger can be tackled easily. Initially it might be tough to get used to it, however, with the passage of time, it does get easier.

You aren't allowed to consume any food during the fasting period. A couple of beverages like coffee and tea are allowed though, in moderation. Some forms of intermittent fasting also provide for the consumption of low-calorie foods in small amounts during the fast period. Supplements can be consumed, provided they don't add any calories.

***

Fasting Throughout the Ages

The concept of fasting isn't a new one. Human beings have been doing this since forever, often out of necessity due to lack of food. Our bodies have been designed in such a way that they can go for long periods of time without any food.

Intermittent fasting is also prominent in all major religions, and is used as a way to humble one self and experience closer intimacy with God:

- **Christianity:** Jesus fasted for forty days and nights in preparation for his ministry.
- **Islam:** During Ramadan, muslims fast from dawn until sunset for one month, to commemorate the revelation of the Quran to Muhammad.
- **Judaism:** The Fast of the Firstborn commemorates the salvation of the Israelite firstborns during the last of the ten plagues, when all Egyptian firstborns were killed. Usually this fast falls on the day before Passover. Interestingly enough, only firstborns are required to fast on this day.
- **Buddhism:** Buddhist monks and nuns practice intermittent fasting every day. They follow the Vinaya rules, a code of discipline laid down by the Buddha himself. One of the rules in this code is to not eat anything after the noon meal.

- **Hinduism:** Fasting is very prominent among hindus. The type of fast, and when it is done, depends on personal belief, as well as which deity one favors.

***

Different Techniques Depending on Needs

There is not just one way of doing a fast. Intermittent fasting might mean different things for different people. In Chapter 3, we will discuss the most common fasting methods.

A little teaser: besides the 16:8 method we just talked about, another common one is the 5:2 method is. If you were following this approach, you would fast for two nonconsecutive days in the week. The rest of the days, there is no restriction on the number of calories that you can consume.

Ultimately, you will perform at your highest level on a fast that best fits your needs and lifestyle.

***

When to Eat, And Not What To Eat

Intermittent fasting is not a diet: there is caloric constraint on those who follow it. The plans for this diet can be personalized quite easily. It focuses more on the time at which you can eat and not what you eat. What matters is that you adhere to the fasting window.

With that being said, it is always good to limit your processed foods intake. Not only is eating junk food not good for your health, it will also worsen your food cravings during the fasting window as you are not giving your body the nutrients it needs. Instead, aim to consume healthy focus on healthy fats (raw nuts, avocados, olive or coconut oil, salmon), proteins (meat, eggs, lentils) and leafy vegetables.

Don't get disheartened if this sounds a bit intense right now. Just try out one method for a while, and if it doesn't work for you, experiment with a different one. You will find one method that works best for you.

***

You Can Consume Beverages, With No Calories

There is one exception when it comes to fasting: you can drink water! All you have been told is to avoid consuming any food with calories in it. You may also drink other liquids like tea and black coffee, as long as it does not contain any calories. That means no cream or sugar!

***

This is the end of this bonus chapter.

You can find the book on the Amazon website, if you would like to continue reading: *'Intermittent Fasting: Burn Fat, Lose Weight And Build Muscle With Ease While Still Eating Your Favorite Foods!'* by Gerard Hamilton.

About The Author

My name is Gerard Hamilton. I am a nutritionist and fitness enthusiast, and I am extremely passionate about health.

Having been overweight myself when I was younger, I know the struggles that many of my readers face every day.

The million-dollar question is: How can you lose weight and enjoy life at the same time?

Well, that is what I am here to teach you!

It is my purpose in life to help you become the best possible version of yourself. This is what makes me come out of bed every morning.

So join me on this journey and let me help you take back control of your health, lose weight and have some fun while we are doing it.

Happy reading!

Made in the USA
Middletown, DE
30 December 2017